T0273066

Three Simple Principles of Trade Policy

Douglas A. Irwin

The AEI Press

Publisher for the American Enterprise Institute

WASHINGTON, D.C.

1996

ISBN 9780-84477-079-6

THE AEI PRESS
Publisher for the American Enterprise Institute
1150 17th Street, N.W., Washington, D.C. 20036

Contents

Acknowledgments

This is a revised version of an informal talk I gave at the American Enterprise Institute in January 1996. I thank AEI President Christopher DeMuth for inviting me to write up my remarks and make them available to a broader audience, as well as for his constructive advice on the text. I also wish to thank Claude Barfield, Jagdish Bhagwati, and Donald Davis for helpful comments.

Introduction

At the conclusion of a class I teach on international commercial policy, I try to distill the essence of a ten-week course down to a few simple principles that students might remember long after the final exam is over. In this essay I expand upon three of these principles.

I have selected these principles with the aim of correcting some common economic fallacies in the political debate over U.S. trade policy. The principles are a bit more subtle, and more pointed, than elementary first principles such as "voluntary exchange is generally beneficial"—a proposition that almost everyone accepts but that rarely settles a practical policy issue. Indeed these principles might seem to be mistaken, on first reading, to many readers whose understanding of trade issues is derived mainly from newpaper accounts—and yet I believe they can be explained persuasively and illustrated with straightforward data and examples that demonstrate their practical relevance.

Most of all, the three principles are offered as examples of important and enduring *knowledge* about international trade, as opposed to the unstructured (or tendentiously structured) *information* about trade that comes our way every day. Each principle is the distillation of generations of serious thinking about the nature of trade among nations—thinking that has endured much longer than the ad hoc arguments and partial information of political debate. This thinking can help us make sense of the information supplied by politicians and interest groups. Major improvements in U.S. trade policy may be out of reach at the present time, but a greater understanding of the three principles offered herein would improve the trade policy debate.

1. A Tax on Imports Is a Tax on Exports

The first proposition is that a tax on imports is equivalent to a tax on exports. Any restraint on imports also acts, in effect, as a restraint on exports. The converse of this proposition is also true: when a government undertakes policies to expand the volume of exports, it cannot help but to expand the volume of imports as well.

The fundamental reason for this truth is that exports and imports are flip sides of the same coin. Exports are necessary to generate the earnings to pay for imports, or exports are the goods a country must give up in order to acquire imports. Exports and imports are inherently interdependent, and any policy that reduces one will also reduce the other.

At one level, the idea that import restraints will reduce exports is simple and straightforward: if foreign countries are blocked in their ability to sell their goods in the United States, for example, they will be unable to earn the dollars they need to purchase U.S. goods. In policy discussions about international trade, however, there is a tendency to view a country's exports and imports as being separate, independent phenomena. In this view, government policy can diminish imports without adversely affecting exports, or vice versa. This view is erroneous because exports and imports do not wander too far from one another. The two are inexorably linked even if the mechanism by which they are linked is not immediately obvious. (Trade imbalances will be considered in proposition 3.)

Before I present some simple data that illustrate this point, let me briefly discuss the intellectual history of this proposition. Economists will recognize it as the "Lerner symmetry theorem," named for the distinguished economist Abba Lerner, who wrote a short but brilliant paper on the subject as a graduate student at the London School of Economics in the mid-1930s.[1] Lerner established the formal truth of the proposition, but it had been a feature of trade policy debates long before then.

The principle was used extensively in the House of Commons in the early 1840s and before, when Parliament was considering whether to repeal the Corn Laws, legislation that limited British grain imports. Members in favor of repeal argued that the import tariffs restrained exports of manufactures, and that allowing greater imports of wheat would lead directly to greater exports of textiles. One Member of Parliament, James Deacon Hume, is recorded as saying that "he did not expect to hear it denied that every import must be paid for by an export. If so, every quarter of wheat imported put into employment some manufacturers to pay for that import."[2]

The symmetry between import and export taxes was recognized even in the seventeenth-century English mercantilist literature. Popular understanding of mercantilist doctrine is that trade barriers were recommended in order to achieve, among other things, a balance of trade surplus. By my reading of this literature, seventeenth-century mercantilist writers certainly wanted to achieve a trade surplus, but they were not at all sanguine about the efficacy of import tariffs in achieving this objective.[3] Even these writers, who rejected free trade as a matter of principle, recognized that exports and imports are fundamentally interdependent. In discussing the tax burden on imports, the pamphleteer Henry Robinson cautioned as early as 1640 that "here is it worth remembrance that a great part of foreign commodities brought for England are taken in barter of ours, and we should not have vented ours in so great quantity without taking them."

In 1680 William Petyt took this point to its logical conclusion:

> For the opening of a sufficient foreign vent and market for our home commodities, it is not only necessary to remove all unequal clogs on mere exportation, but also those on imported goods;

> because . . . the value of our English exporta-
> tion must be in a manner confined to the value of
> the goods imported. . . . Whereas were the clogs
> on our imported goods taken off, we might yearly
> vend of our own home commodities to the value
> of all foreign goods we should then import and
> re-export. . . whereby our exported home com-
> modities would then amount to much more.[4]

Recognition of the interdependence of exports and imports put mercantilists in a bind because import tariffs
appeared to be the obvious instrument for improving the
balance of trade by reducing imports without directly affecting exports. Thus, the Lerner symmetry theorem has
a long intellectual pedigree.

Lerner's Symmetry: True and Nontrivial. What is particularly marvelous about the Lerner symmetry theorem is that
it is both true and nontrivial. (In this regard it is like another fundamental principle of international trade: the
theory of comparative advantage.) The equivalence of
export and import taxes is not an obvious proposition,
and it is often counterintuitive to most people. Imagine
taking a poll of average Americans and asking the following question: "Should the United States impose import
tariffs on foreign textiles to prevent low-wage countries
from harming thousands of American textile workers?"
Some fraction, perhaps even a sizeable one, of the respon-
dents would surely answer affirmatively. If asked to explain
their position, they would probably reply that import tariffs would create jobs for Americans at the expense of foreign workers and thereby reduce domestic unemployment.

Suppose you then asked those same people the following question: "Should the United States tax the expor-
tation of Boeing aircraft, wheat and corn, computers and
computer software, and other domestically produced
goods?" I suspect the answer would be a resounding and

unanimous "No!" After all, it would be explained, export taxes would destroy jobs and harm important industries. And yet the Lerner symmetry theorem says that the two policies are equivalent in their economic effects.

This all goes to show that the issue of tax incidence is a tricky one. One may think that an import tariff is felt only in the import sector, but in the end this is not the case. Because the economic equivalency of export and import taxation is not intuitive, clearly they are unlikely to be considered equivalent in the political arena. The Founding Fathers, for example, wrote into the Constitution (Article I, Section 9) a prohibition of export taxes, but the first act of the first Congress was the imposition of an import tariff. Because of this political nonequivalence, I doubt that things would have been much different even if the Founding Fathers had been aware of the Lerner symmetry theorem.

How can the equivalence proposition be true? One aspect of the answer is that both policies drive domestic resource allocation in the same direction. If the United States produces textiles (which face import competition) and aircraft (which can be exported), an import tariff raises the domestic price of textiles and attracts factors of production from the aircraft industry and elsewhere to the textile industry in order to increase output. An export tax reduces the reward to producing aircraft and shifts productive factors away from that sector toward the production of textiles and other goods. This highly simplified example makes the point that taxes on trade—either imports or exports—move the economy away from producing exported goods and toward producing more import-competing goods. Yet this example fails to drive home the point completely because it is not obvious how an import restriction in a particular sector (as opposed to an across-the-board measure) will redound to the loss of some particular exporter.

So what mechanisms specifically link a country's exports and imports to one another? The mechanisms can be complex and subtle, but focusing on the foreign exchange market can perhaps illuminate what is going on. If the United States unilaterally reduces its tariff on Japanese goods, for example, one would expect U.S. demand for Japanese goods to increase. In this case, consumers in the United States will (indirectly) have to sell dollars on the foreign exchange market to purchase yen. This tends to depress the value of the dollar in terms of the yen or, conversely, to raise the value of the yen in terms of the dollar. The depreciation of the dollar tends to raise the price of Japanese goods in the United States, dampening demand for those goods.

But here is the flip side: even though Japan did not change its tariff on U.S. goods, Japan will now purchase more goods from the United States because the depreciated dollar will tend to lower the yen price of U.S. goods. In other words, the foreign exchange market is one mechanism that links exports and imports to ensure that when a country unilaterally reduces its tariff its exports increase as well.[5] While this is a highly simplistic example and can be subject to various qualifications in practice, it is nonetheless a useful thought experiment. In most cases, one cannot directly observe the mechanism by which exports and imports are linked. Although the effect is not obvious or overt, it is still present and operative.

Evidence of Symmetry. The data support the theory. The past century of experience for the United States should be sufficient to illustrate the close relationship between exports and imports. Figure 1 plots U.S. exports and imports from 1895 to 1995. Because the nominal value of exports and imports explode from the early 1970s from inflation, the trade deficit of the 1980s becomes exaggerated relative to earlier periods. Hence, the log of exports and imports—to indicate proportionate changes—is presented.

Exports and imports are unmistakably correlated:

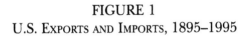

FIGURE 1

U.S. Exports and Imports, 1895–1995

Log of Exports and Imports

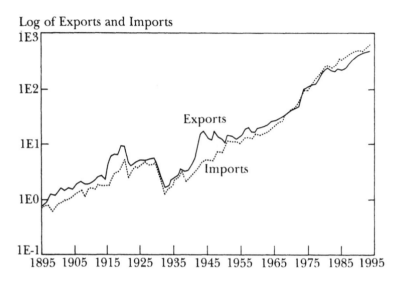

Sources: U.S. Department of Commerce, *Historical Statistics of the United States* (U.S. GPO, 1975); *Economic Report of the President* (U.S. GPO, 1996).

they rise and fall in lockstep, such that one cannot distinguish between them. Revisionists about U.S. economic policies during the postwar period have complained that it was marked by a one-sided opening of the U.S. market; foreign trade barriers and unfair practices, they charge, were tolerated far too long. Yet the openness of the U.S. market does not manifest itself in a differential in the levels of exports or imports.

More evidence comes from the recent experience of developing countries. Figure 2 depicts exports and imports as a percentage of gross domestic product (GDP) for two years, 1965 and 1990, for four developing countries—India, Brazil, South Korea, and Chile, countries that practiced starkly different commercial policies over this period.

7

FIGURE 2
EXPORTS AND IMPORTS AS SHARE OF GDP, INDIA, BRAZIL, SOUTH KOREA, AND CHILE, 1965 AND 1990

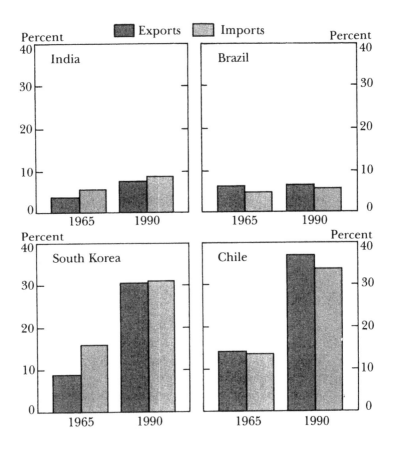

SOURCE: International Monetary Fund, *International Financial Statistics, Yearbook 1995.*

India and Brazil have pursued classic "import substitution" policies, which aimed to promote industrialization by severely restricting imports—not just through tariffs and quotas but also through import licensing requirements and foreign exchange restrictions. In 1965, exports and imports amounted to less than 10 percent of GDP for both countries. Their trade policies did not change substantially in the intervening twenty-five years, and thus their exports and imports still remained less than 10 percent of GDP in 1990. Despite the desire of India and Brazil to expand exports, they were constrained by the fact that during this period they maintained substantial import barriers. These import taxes acted as a tax on exports.

Contrast this experience with that of South Korea and Chile. These countries pursued quite different policies not only from India and Brazil but also from each other. Korea is well known for its export promotion policies that encouraged firms to produce for the world market. In 1965, Korea's exports amounted to less than 10 percent of GDP, just like India and Brazil. By 1990 exports amounted to more than 30 percent of GDP. At the same time, Korea is not well known for having liberalized its home market to imports, and many regard it still as a market difficult to penetrate, if not largely closed to foreign goods. Yet imports also grew to more than 30 percent of GDP. An export push led to an import surge.

Unlike Korea, Chile is not usually associated with any targeted policies to promote exports. Instead, one thinks of the extensive deregulation and trade liberalization of the 1970s that reduced tariffs and quotas and other government restrictions on imports. Partly as a result, Chile's imports surged from under 15 percent of GDP in 1965 to nearly 35 percent in 1990. Yet this period also witnessed a surge in exports on the same order of magnitude. An expansion of imports was matched by an expansion of exports.

This illustrates the functional importance of the Lerner symmetry theorem. It is not just a hypothetical abstraction. If a government undertakes policies that systematically reduce the volume of imports, it also systematically reduces the volume of exports. The reasons may be indirect and less than obvious, but they are still present and have to be reckoned with.

2. Businesses Are Consumers Too

In his celebrated attack on mercantilism, Adam Smith elevated the role of the consumer in economic affairs by writing: "Consumption is the sole end and purpose of all production; and the interests of the producer ought to be attended to, only so far as it may be necessary for promoting that of the consumer." Smith criticized government policies for neglecting this point and even reversing this ordering: "But in the mercantile system, the interest of the consumer is almost constantly sacrificed to that of the producer; and it seems to consider production, and not consumption, as the ultimate end and object of all industry and commerce." [6] Adam Smith argued that countries like consumers should thus seek out the lowest price in the market through free trade: "What is prudence in the conduct of every private family, can scarce be folly in that of a great kingdom." [7]

The image conveyed by Smith as well as by later economists is straightforward: the consumer is a household. The consumer is one of us, acting in the role of purchaser of goods, whether in the supermarket, the shopping mall, or elsewhere. Because protection raises the price of goods purchased by the consumer, that policy is antithetical to the interests of the consumer. This imagery and analogy serve the purpose of getting the reader to identify with the consumer, since in fact each of us is one.

The Consumer Cost Argument. Since then, economists have always stressed the costs to consumers of various trade restrictions in terms of the higher price they must pay as a result. In writing against the Corn Laws in 1825, John Stuart Mill objected that protection robbed consumers and, what is worse, was a wasteful transfer of resources because consumers had to pay more than producers received in benefits, resulting in a deadweight loss to society. "If there were nothing in the whole process but a transfer; if whatever is lost by the consumer and by the capitalist were gains by the landlord; there might be robbery, but there would not be waste. . . . For every pound which finds its way into the pockets of the landlords, . . . the community is robbed of several." [8] Economists have continued, correctly, to point out the often substantial consumer costs of trade protection. The best recent illustration is the Multi-Fiber Arrangement (MFA), which has been called the biggest piece of protectionist cholesterol blocking the arteries of world trade today. (The recently concluded Uruguay Round of trade negotiations, though, promises to end it in a decade.) The MFA restricts the importation of foreign textiles and apparel and results in significantly higher prices to U.S. consumers for clothing. Hufbauer and Elliot estimate the consumer cost of this protection as $24.4 billion in 1990, a burden amounting to more than $260 per U.S. household.[9] The tax is quite regressive, because households with lower incomes devote a greater share of their expenditures to clothing than those with higher incomes. The MFA is also an extremely costly employment program. Hufbauer and Elliot calculate that the consumer cost amounts to $144,751 per job saved in the textile and apparel industry, merely to keep workers employed in relatively low-skill, low-wage occupations.

Another example is the "voluntary export restraint" (VER) adopted by Japan (under U.S. pressure) in 1981 to reduce its automobile exports to the United States. The effect on consumers was quite stark and unambiguous: according to most estimates, the average cost of an automobile rose more than $1,000 as a result of the trade restriction. While one can always quarrel with the particulars of these numbers, the rough magnitude of these consumer cost figures is difficult to dispute, and the burden they impose is not to be belittled. The costs are real and should be brought to the public's attention.

Those favoring free trade, however, use the consumer cost argument almost as an automatic reflex: because the price to consumers will rise as a result of a proposed trade intervention, the policy is deemed unwise. Yet there is a problem with pushing the "consumer cost of protection" argument too much. Aside from the fact that it has been used so often that it sounds a bit stale by now, the refrain can even appear whiny in the face of genuine economic distress. Industries usually press for import restrictions only when they are suffering from a serious competitive threat, sometimes for reasons quite outside their control, such as the sizeable appreciation of the dollar in the early 1980s. To dismiss that suffering in this age of (at least perceived) economic insecurity by saying "it's a bad idea for consumers to pay more," or "if our industry cannot hack the competition we should let it go," sounds bloodless and unfeeling, or implies that free traders are elevating "consumerism" over the claims of good jobs and industrial strength. To be sure, the image of well-paid (by the standards of other manufacturing workers) automobile workers and executives from industries operating at near full capacity complaining about foreign competition is galling. But this, of course, is not always the case.

The real problem is not that the mantra of the "consumer cost of protection" argument is wrong but that it has failed in the political arena. Economists grind out countless figures for what consumers will pay if some trade restriction is imposed, including an outrageously high cost per job saved, and yet these figures do not cause much stir in the political debate. The numbers sound much too abstract to have an effect. In addition, jobs are viewed as being much more important than consumer welfare in the political arena. If the question comes down to saving a few hundred jobs in some industry or saving consumers a few hundred dollars in income, the policy of import protection will win every time.

This unequal weighting of jobs and consumer income is attributable partly to classic political economy reasons: producer interests are concentrated and hence well represented politically, while consumers' costs are spread over

TABLE 1
U.S. IMPORTS BY END-USE CATEGORY, 1929–1994
(percentage distribution)

	Consumer Goods	Industrial Supplies and Materials	Capital Goods
1929	33.9	65.2	0.9
1950	36.4	62.4	1.3
1970	45.5	37.8	13.2
1990	39.1	30.1	30.8
1994	38.8	25.5	35.6

NOTE: Figures may not sum to 100, because of rounding.
SOURCES: For 1929 and 1950, U.S. Office of Business Economics, *U.S. Exports and Imports Classified by OBE End-Use Commodity Categories, 1923–68* (Supplement to the *Survey of Current Business,* November 1970). For 1970, 1990, 1994, *Survey of Current Business,* March issue of year after date.

millions of households that simply do not have the incentive to undertake any effort to reverse the policy. Another cause is perception: jobs are viewed as being the *source* of consumer income. There is so much political concern about employment that those in favor of free trade who trot out only the consumer cost argument will have the following thrown back at them: "Without jobs there would be no consumer income; therefore protection is a small price to pay for greater employment in industry *X*."

The Burden on Downstream Industries. To overcome this stalemate, I propose that the consumer-cost-of-protection argument be augmented by the following observation: businesses are consumers too. I believe that this simple change can go a long way in leveling the playing field between those who want some form of trade protection and those who do not.

Business firms are, in fact, bigger consumers of imported products than are U.S. households. The U.S. Department of Commerce publishes data on U.S. imports by end-use classification, wherein they attempt to determine what the imports are actually used for. Table 1 shows this distribution for various years since 1929. The three categories are consumer goods, industrial supplies and materials, and capital goods. Consumer goods include foods, feeds, and beverages, assembled automobiles, and consumer durables and nondurables. Industrial supplies and materials include crude and processed materials, such as fuels and lubricants, paper, building materials, and so forth. Capital goods include machinery, equipment, apparatus, and instruments, as well as parts, components, and accessories, including automobile parts.

Industrial materials and captial goods are, for the most part, not sold directly to households but to business firms as an input into their production process. Table 1 indicates that more than 60 percent of U.S. imports are intermediate components or raw materials that are inputs to production, not final consumer goods. How does recognition of this fact affect our thinking about trade policy and alter the political debate over the desirability of intervention?

One can go down the list of trade policy interventions over the past two decades and see that many of the commodities at issue constitute intermediate goods. Any trade intervention that raises the price of an intermediate good will at some point adversely affect most households as final consumers. But the immediate adverse effect is on other downstream user industries and, necessarily, employment in those industries. Thus, a clear link can be established between import protection and job losses in other industries. If one can augment the statement that protection will cost consumers more with the message that it will reduce employment in related industries, one has a politically more potent argument.

U.S. steel policy provides a good example. In 1984, the Reagan administration announced major voluntary restraint agreements (VRAs) involving import limits on all major foreign suppliers of steel. The VRAs kept the price of steel in the United States higher than it would otherwise have been, to the detriment of steel-using industries. An ad hoc organization of these downstream industries formed the Coalition of American Steel-Using Manufacturers (CASUM) to oppose renewal of the VRAs. CASUM was headed by Caterpillar, the manufacturer of heavy earthmoving equipment and a major steel-using concern, and the Precision Metalforming Association, a small business group whose members process raw steel for industrial users such as the automobile industry.

CASUM opposed steel protection on the grounds that, by raising U.S. steel prices, it adversely affected the production, employment, and exports of the far more numerous domestic steel-using industries. As Michael Moore notes, "the overall strategy of CASUM was to turn the debate away from the actions of foreign firms and governments and away from an argument about free trade versus protection. Instead, CASUM tried to direct the discussion toward the effects of the VRAs on U.S. manufacturing interests, especially exporters and small businesses. This was a highly effective tactic, since both have broad political support."[10] In other words, Caterpillar was able to ask: "How are we supposed to compete at home and abroad against such foreign competitors as Komatsu when we are forced to pay a hefty premium for the steel that is needed as an input to production?" Needless to say, trade authorities would have difficulty answering that question. If Caterpillar is forced to lay off workers because of lost sales to offshore producers, those unemployed could rightfully ask: Does the government really believe that jobs in the steel industry are more important to the economy than jobs in the equipment manufacturing industry?

The United States has also maintained tight quotas on sugar imports, which have pushed the U.S. price of sugar up to two and sometime three times the world price.

While U.S. consumers pay more for a bag of sugar at the grocery store as a result, the real effect has been on sugar-using industries. Food manufacturers who produce sugar-intensive products have to pay a higher price for this input than do their foreign rivals, and as a result they are less competitive against imported and domestic substitutes. James Bovard reports that the U.S. Department of Commerce estimates that almost 9,000 jobs in food manufacturing were lost as a result of the high price of sugar in the mid-1980s.[11] Brachs Candy Company, for example, announced in 1990 that because of the high price of sugar in the United States it would close a factory in Chicago that employed 3,000 workers and would expand production in Canada. The United States, according to Bovard, has only 11,000 sugar farmers, but more than 7,000 jobs in the sugar refining industry have been lost as imports have been squeezed out.

This adverse effect of protection on downstream industries is also evident in the high-technology sector. The United States reached an antidumping agreement concerning DRAM (dynamic random access memory) semiconductors with Japan in the mid-1980s that resulted in a dramatic price increase in the U.S. market. These higher prices severely harmed the competitive position of DRAM-users, particularly computer manufacturers who had to compete against foreign rivals that had the benefit of much lower memory chip prices. Led by IBM, Tandem, and Hewlett-Packard, several of these firms formed the Computer Systems Policy Project (CSPP) to counter the lobbying power of the Semiconductor Industry Association (SIA). The CSPP complained that the United States had become a "high price island" of semiconductors and threatened to move computer production to southeast Asia to take advantage of lower semiconductor prices. When the United States later imposed antidumping duties on imports of flat panel displays, domestic manufacturers that used those screens stated that they also could not com-

16

pete if forced to pay higher prices in the United States and would shift production abroad, where prices were lower.

By viewing imports not as final consumer goods but as inputs to U.S. production, policy makers can more clearly recognize that the issue is not so much one of "saving" jobs but of "trading off" jobs between sectors. This brings home forcefully the most important lesson in all of economics—there is no such thing as a free lunch. Every action involves a trade-off of some sort. Higher domestic steel prices help employment in the steel industry but harm employment in steel-using industries. Higher domestic semiconductor prices help employment in the semiconductor industry but harm employment in semiconductor-using industries. As John Stuart Mill wrote in 1848 in the context of import protection, "The alternative is not between employing our own country-people and foreigners, but between employing one class or another of our own country-people."[12]

3. Trade Imbalances Reflect Capital Flows

The field of international finance has traditionally addressed the determinants of a country's current account balance, the broadest measure of trade in merchandise goods and services. Trade policy debates, however, are so bound up with concerns about trade imbalances that often these international finance issues cannot be considered separately from commercial policy.

One of the main lessons of international finance is that trade imbalances reflect net capital flows between countries.[13] This point was emphasized repeatedly by economists in the 1980s, when the U.S. current account moved sharply into deficit. Yet this lesson is still apparently lost on many policy officials today, as when one hears that the United States suffers a trade deficit because its market is more open than those of other countries, or that Japan has a trade surplus because its market is closed to imports. The United States may have a relatively open market and foreign markets may be more closed, but these facts would not manifest themselves in the trade balance.

The Balance of Payments. Any analysis of trade imbalances must begin with the general balance of payments. The balance of payments is simply an accounting of a country's international transactions. Balance-of-payments accounting is a very dry subject, but some familiarity with it would take away much of the mystery of what a trade deficit is and what its underlying causes are. It would also indicate which remedies are likely to be effective or ineffective in correcting such a deficit, should that course of action be considered desirable.

The first accounting lesson is this: the balance of payments always balances—that is, sums to zero. This is an accounting identity, which is to say that it holds by definition.[14] Two broad categories of transactions enter into the balance of payments—the *current account*, which records all trade in merchandise goods and services, and the *capi-*

tal account, which records all trade in assets, either portfolio or direct investments. Because the balance of payments always balances, a country running a current account deficit must also have a counterbalancing capital account surplus. In other words, if a country is buying more goods and services from the rest of the world than it is selling, the country must also be selling more assets to the rest of the world than it is buying.

This necessary link might become clearer by considering the case of an individual. If, in a given year, an individual's expenditures exactly match his or her income, the net asset position of that individual would not change (i.e., there would be no accumulation or decumulation of assets, and no net borrowing or lending vis-à-vis the rest of the economy). Can a person buy more in goods and services in a given year than he or she sells to others in earning an income? Of course, in one of two ways: either by borrowing to make up the difference or by selling previously held assets to finance the difference. Either method reduces the individual's net asset position and amounts to his or her becoming a net borrower in that year.

Countries finance their current account imbalances in exactly the same way. Thus, suppose a U.S. firm purchases a component from a South Korean firm for $100. Ignoring all other transactions for the moment, the United States now has a $100 trade deficit with Korea. But what does the Korean firm do with the $100? If the firm uses it to purchase a U.S. good, the trade deficit disappears. Alternatively, the firm (or anyone to whom the firm sells the dollars) can acquire assets in the United States, such as by depositing the $100 in a U.S. bank account or by purchasing $100 worth of U.S. stock. Both of these transactions are recorded as positive entries in the U.S. capital account, increases in U.S. liabilities to foreigners. In this case, therefore, the United States was in effect borrowing from or selling assets to Korea in order to finance the purchase of Korean goods. Countries with current account deficits are effectively borrowing from or selling assets to other countries. Countries with current account surpluses, by contrast, are buying assets from the rest of the world, or using their savings to act as net lenders to other countries.

There is a fundamental equation of international finance that relates this net borrowing and lending activity to the current account. The equation is:

$$\text{Exports} - \text{Imports} = \text{Savings} - \text{Investment}.$$

In other words, countries running trade surpluses (the value of their exports exceeding the value of their imports) have domestic savings in excess of domestic investment. This "excess" savings, which is invested or lent abroad, manifests itself in a capital account deficit, the counterpart of which is a current account surplus. Countries with trade deficits can sustain greater domestic investment than domestic savings because of the addition of foreign savings, which come in as a capital account surplus, or current account deficit.

The powerful implication of this equation is that if a country wishes to reduce its trade deficit, the gap between its domestic investment and its domestic savings must be reduced. Unless a nation's trade policies also affect its total savings or investment, those policies will be ineffective in altering its balance of trade. That is why simple observation shows us that some countries with open markets run trade surpluses and others run trade deficits, while some countries with closed markets run trade surpluses and others run trade deficits. Those imbalances have everything to do with international borrowing and lending and virtually nothing to do with commercial policy.

A government's borrowing to cover a fiscal deficit can be one of the largest drains on a country's savings and can therefore lead to a current account deficit. One reason for the large U.S. current account deficit in the early 1980s was the rapid increase in the government's fiscal deficit. The lesson is that fiscal retrenchment can reverse a country's trade imbalance. As the U.S. government's annual fiscal deficit shrank from 4.7 percent to 2.4 percent of GDP between 1986 and 1989 (from roughly $200 billion to $124 billion

FIGURE 3
CURRENT ACCOUNT BALANCES OF THE UNITED STATES, JAPAN, AND GERMANY, 1956–1994

A. United States

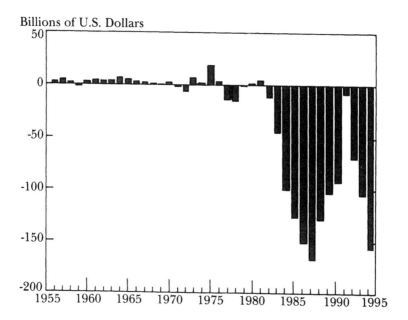

(Figure continues)

in nominal terms), for example, the deficit on trade in goods and services also fell from 3.1 percent to 1.6 percent of GDP.[15]

Capital Mobility and the Current Account. The ability of a country to run a current account surplus or deficit depends on the degree to which countries allow capital to move between them. This in turn is a function of the international monetary system and the particular exchange rate regime in place. In the absence of international capi-

FIGURE 3
(continued)

B. Japan

Billions of U.S. Dollars

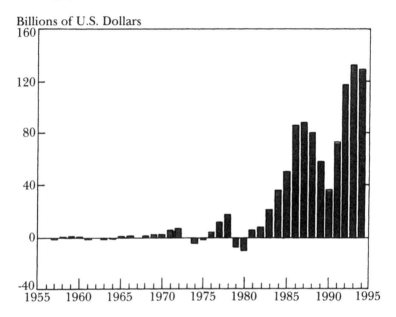

tal mobility, that is, of international borrowing and lending, domestic savings equals domestic investment, and therefore trade is balanced as exports equal imports.

During the classical gold standard from about 1880–1913, by contrast, international capital flows were largely unrestricted. All national monies were based on gold, and there were no restrictions on the export or import of gold. This period witnessed large net flows of capital between countries as savings spilled out of the London financial markets to be invested in the United States, Canada, Australia, Argentina, and other developing countries of that period. The United Kingdom was a net lender to the rest of the world, experiencing very large current account surpluses (as a percentage of GNP) by today's stan-

FIGURE 3
(continued)

C. Germany

Billions of U.S. Dollars

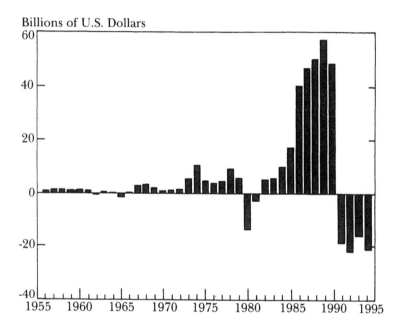

SOURCE: International Monetary Fund, *International Finance Statistics, Yearbook 1995.*

dards. The United States ran current account deficits around 1.0 percent of GNP (amounting to 5.6 percent of domestic investment) from 1884 –1893 as British investors purchased assets such as railroad bonds sold in New York.[16]

Under the Bretton Woods system of fixed exchange rates, which lasted roughly from 1950 to 1973, a quite different state of affairs prevailed. To maintain fixed exchange rates (when monies were not backed by a commodity such as gold), governments restricted international capital mobility through a series of controls on capital movements. Although there were some (in retrospect relatively minor) net capital flows related to direct foreign investments, portfolio capital transactions were minimal by current standards. If little net borrowing or lending activity between countries is permitted, then capital accounts will remain roughly in balance, implying in turn that current accounts will be balanced. If the international monetary system is one that suppresses and discourages capital account transactions, then it should be no surprise that countries also achieved balanced current accounts.

Note that these balanced current accounts have nothing to do with whether or not a country is open to foreign goods, has unfair trade practices, or is more productive or competitive than other countries. If net capital flows are zero, the current account will be balanced.

Figure 3 illustrates this point. This figure depicts the current account balances of the United States, Japan, and Germany for the period 1956–1994. The United States achieved close to current account balance through the 1950s and 1960s, the heyday of the Bretton Woods system, despite the fact that it had an overwhelming economic superiority over Japan and Germany, which had been devastated by World War II. If the current account, whose largest constituent item is the merchandise trade balance, was determined by productive advantages, then the United States should have experienced large surpluses.

Japan and Germany also had roughly balanced current accounts during this period. If the Japanese market is said to be closed now, it was locked shut during this earlier period with extensive government restrictions on imports through tariffs, quotas, prior-approval requirements, and foreign investment controls. Yet just because Japan had a closed market and it successfully exported first textiles and then consumer electronics in the 1950s and 1960s did not mean that it achieved current account surpluses.

Even into the 1970s, these countries maintained roughly balanced current accounts. But why, as the figure makes clear, did all of this change so dramatically in the 1980s? After the collapse of the Bretton Woods system in the early 1970s, the major currencies were permitted to float against one another. Since the purpose of capital controls was to enable governments to maintain fixed exchange rates, the advent of market-determined floating exchange rates rendered those controls unnecessary. Although the United States, as the reserve currency under the Bretton Woods system, had few capital controls in place, most other countries did have them. Those countries gradually phased out their controls on international capital movements over the 1970s and the early 1980s.

Japan, for example, passed the Foreign Exchange and Foreign Trade Control Law in December 1980, which eased restrictions on the holding of foreign assets by Japanese investors. When the barriers were lifted, the large pool of savings that Japan had built up over the years, which had been earning relatively low rates of return in domestic investments, sloshed onto world capital markets in search of higher returns. Japan did this precisely at the time when U.S. real interest rates were high and the U.S. government was selling Treasury bills to finance its growing fiscal deficit. Japan thus became a major purchaser of foreign assets and, as such, served as a net lender to the rest of the world.

As Japan was purchasing more assets than it was selling to foreigners, it ran a large capital account deficit. The converse of this was a large current account surplus, which shifted from an $11 billion deficit in 1980 to a $21 billion surplus in 1983 (and peaked at $87 billion in 1987). In essence, most of the dollars that the United States was handing over to purchase Japanese goods were used by Japan not to purchase an equivalent U.S. good but rather a U.S. asset. It did so because Japanese investors were now permitted to do what they had previously been prevented from doing: making productive investments in the United States that promised to yield higher rates of return. Japan's current account surplus grew not because it had a closed market, not because the United States had an open market, not because Japanese manufacturers had become more "competitive," but mainly for financial and macroeconomic reasons coinciding with the lifting of capital controls in the early 1980s.[17]

Germany also served as a net lender to the rest of the world throughout much of the 1970s and 1980s. But what happened so suddenly in 1991? Germany's current account position swung from a nearly $50 billion surplus in 1990 to a nearly $20 billion deficit in 1991. As in Japan's case, this swift, massive reversal was unrelated to trade policy or competitiveness. It was caused by German reunification, which opened up large investment opportunities in Eastern Germany. In addition, the German government increased its borrowing to finance enormous fiscal transfers to the east. As a result, Germany became a net borrower from the rest of the world: more foreign capital began to move into Germany and less German capital was moving out.

What is the bottom line? A country's trade balance is related to international capital flows—not with open or closed markets, unfair trade practices, or national competitiveness. If a country wants to solve the "problem" of its trade deficit, it must reverse the international flow of capital into its country. In many cases net foreign borrowing can be reversed by reducing the government fiscal deficit. Of course, capital controls could also achieve this purpose, as in the Bretton Woods period; but rather than suppress the movement of capital itself, policy makers should respond to the underlying economic forces generating the capital movement.

Conclusion

These three simple principles of trade policy, and the ideas behind them, are not new (some have been debated for more than 400 years) and are not today controversial among international economists. Having stood the test of time, they come as close to *truths* as anything economists have to offer in any area of policy controversy. Yet they are routinely denied, explicitly or implicitly, in trade policy debates in the United States and elsewhere. I do not imagine that a greater appreciation of these principles would invariably bring about more liberal trade policies; I offer them, rather, in the more modest hope that they might lead to sounder debates in which the real consequences of government policies are confronted more seriously than at present.

Notes

1. See A. P. Lerner, "The Symmetry between Import and Export Taxes," *Economica* 3 n.s. (August 1936), pp. 306–13.

2. *Parliamentary Debates,* vol. 18, May 17, 1833, p. 1,359.

3. My reading is set out in chapter 3 of Douglas A. Irwin, *Against the Tide: An Intellectual History of Free Trade* (Princeton: Princeton University Press, 1996).

4. Another writer concurred, arguing in 1704 that high duties are "only an expedient, but no cure" to the problem of excessive imports, and that "duties are a violence upon trade" which "must, in the course of trade, lessen our own exportations." All quotes are from Irwin, *Against the Tide.*

5. Because only a small fraction of foreign exchange transactions are undertaken to finance international trade, exchange rates are determined in asset markets and may not always act to balance trade as this simple example implies.

6. Adam Smith, *An Inquiry into the Nature and Causes of the Wealth of Nations,* Glasgow Edition of the Works and Correspondence of Adam Smith (Oxford: Clarendon Press, 1976), vol. II, p. 660.

7. Ibid, vol. I, p. 457.

8. John Stuart Mill, "The Corn Law," *Westminster Review* 3 (April 1825), p. 399.

9. Gary C. Hufbauer and Kimberly A. Elliot, *Measuring the Costs of Protection in the United States* (Washington, D.C.: Institute for International Economics, 1994), p. 15..

10. Moore also writes that "CASUM also appealed indirectly to protectionist elements in Congress by emphasizing that VRAs rewarded unfair traders through the transfer of quota rents;" that is, foreign firms got the benefit of selling at higher prices in the U.S. market. Michael O. Moore, "Steel Protection in the 1980s: The Waning Influence of Big Steel?" In *The Political Economy of American Trade Policy,* ed. Anne O. Krueger (Chicago: University of Chicago Press, 1996), pp. 111–12.

11. James Bovard, *The Fair Trade Fraud* (New York: St. Martin's Press, 1991), p. 75..

12. Quoted in Irwin, *Against the Tide,* pp. 36–7.

13. Discussion of this issue predates by decades David Hume's famous argument in the 1750s that the mercantilist pursuit of perpetual trade surpluses was self-defeating because of offsetting gold flows. See ibid., pp. 49–50.

14. A country therefore cannot experience a "balance of payments deficit" unless one is using the old nomenclature that considers official reserve transactions (an important component of the balance of payments under fixed exchange rate regimes) as a separate part of the international accounts.

15. Calculated from the *Economic Report of the President* (1996).

16. See Robert E. Lipsey, "U.S. Foreign Trade and the Balance of Payments, 1800–1913," Working paper no. 4710, National Bureau of Economic Research, April 1994.

17. The yen-dollar exchange rate, which was driven in part by capital flows, was a mechanism that played a key role in bringing about the current account deficit.

About the Author

Douglas A. Irwin is the Henry Wendt Scholar in Political Economy at the American Enterprise Institute. He is also an associate professor of business economics at the University of Chicago's Graduate School of Business and a faculty research fellow of the National Bureau of Economic Research. He is author of *Against the Tide: An Intellectual History of Free Trade* (1996) and *Managed Trade: The Case against Import Targets* (AEI Press, 1994).

www.ingramcontent.com/pod-product-compliance
Lightning Source LLC
Jackson TN
JSHW011944131224
75386JS00041B/1558